mel bay's

third position easy & melodic violin etudes

by stephanie hack swoveland

1 2 3 4 5 6 7 8 9 0

Table of Contents

Introduction

The purpose of this book is to provide students and teachers with an enjoyable, fast-paced and effective means to learn the third position. This studio tested book will encourage students to try and continue to use third position.

This book is designed to facilitate third position use with visual, aural and technical ease. Visually, enlarged staves and notes make technical difficulties seem easier. Scale finger pattern diagrams start students off with a clear plan for finger placement. Aurally, the melodies are simple and easy to remember, encouraging learning by ear. Technically, shifts are limited, repetitive and systematic.

The keys chosen for study are those that easily start a foundation for shifting skills. Scales, finger patterns and a variety of exercises are included. Students are often surprised by how easily they execute the three octave G major scale and etude.

This book is intended for group or private lesson use in school music programs, Suzuki and traditional lesson studios. Students will enjoy using this book because they get satisfaction and a boost of confidence when they experience quick success.

Suggestions from the Author

- I. Review perfected pages as a warm up to reinforce developing skills.
- II. Play etudes or etude sections in first position to help establish pitches by ear.
- III. Check open string pitches with open strings. Listen for a ringing sound when the notes are in tune.
- IV. Slide gently and slowly at first. Do not slide beyond the correct pitch.
- V. Keep the bow firmly into the string on shifts.
- VI. Keep the bow from slipping toward the fingerboard when shifting with fingers.
- VII. Start all pieces in a slow tempo. As each piece is mastered, follow tempo markings.
- VIII. Maintain a full, clear tone at all times.

About the Author

Stephanie Hack Swoveland has a Master of Music degree in Performance and Pedagogy from the University of Houston, a Music Teaching Certificate from Carnegie Mellon University, and a B.A. in Music from the University of South Florida. She has studied performance and teaching techniques in a college laboratory Suzuki program, the Meadowmount School and the Aspen Music Festival. She has performed with symphony, ballet and opera orchestras, shows and various ensembles in the United States, Canada and Europe. She currently maintains her own music studio in Pittsburgh, PA and teaches at the Center for the Musically Talented in the Pittsburgh Public School System.

The D Major Scale
Two Octaves

The key of D Major has two sharps: F♯ and C♯.

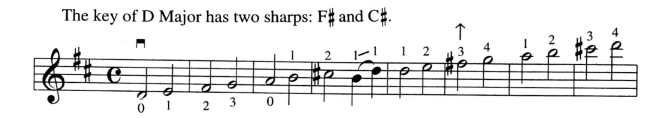

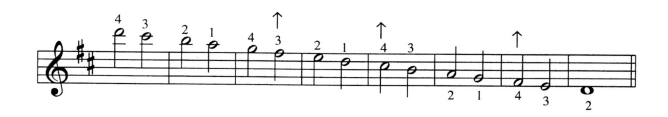

Third Position Finger Pattern

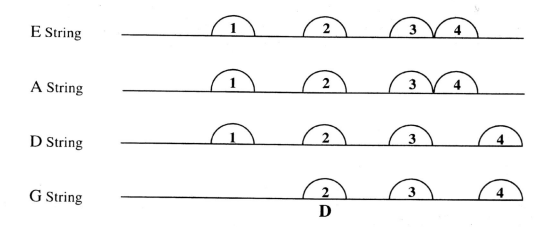

Write the name near each note:
On the scale notes and the finger pattern.

Etude No. 1 in D Major

Moderato

Swoveland

Etude No. 2 in D Major

Moderato

Swoveland

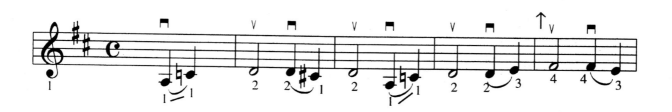

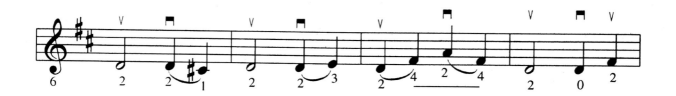

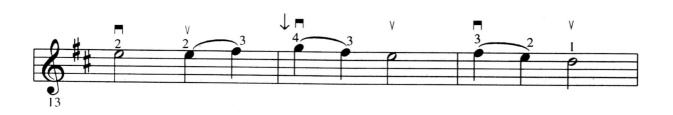

Third Position Twinkle, Twinkle, Little Star
in D Major

Moderato

Traditional
Arr. Swoveland

Variation 1

Moderato

Swoveland

Variation 2

Moderato

Swoveland

Variation 3

Moderato

Swoveland

Variation 4

Moderato

Swoveland

12

Variation 5

Moderato

Swoveland

Variation 6

Moderato

Swoveland

The D Minor Scale
One Octave

The D Melodic Minor key has: Ascending B♮ and C♯
Descending B♭ and C♮.

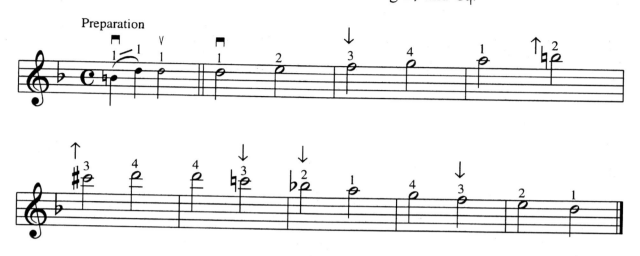

Third Position Finger Pattern

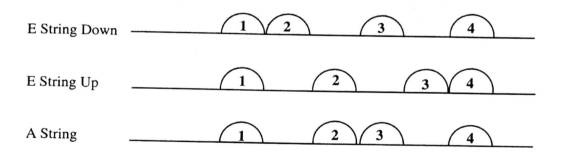

Write the name near each note:
On the scale notes and the finger pattern.

Etude in D Minor

Slowly

Swoveland

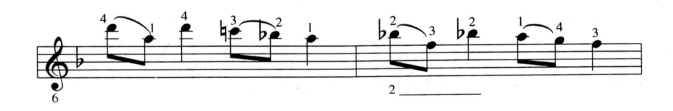

Near each note, write the name of the
string on which you are bowing.

Name and Play Each Note

Name and Play Each Note
Use the Third Position Fingering Given

The C Major Scale in Third Position
Two Octaves

The key of C Major has no sharps and no flats.

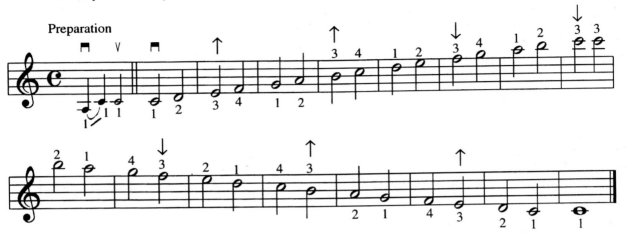

Third Position Finger Pattern

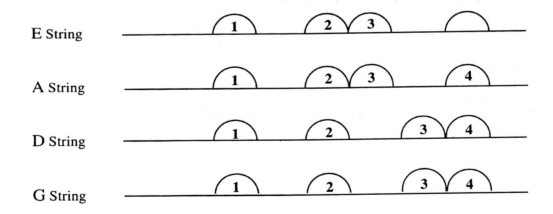

Say each note's name as you play it.

Etude No. 1 in C Major

Moderato

Swoveland

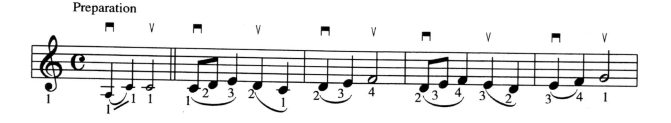

Etude No. 2 in C Major

Adagio

Swoveland

The F Major Scale
One Octave

The key of F Major has one flat: B♭.

First Position

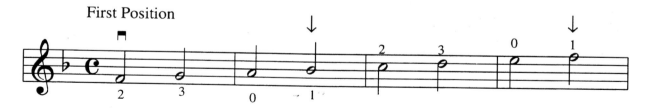

Third Position

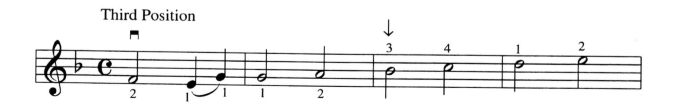

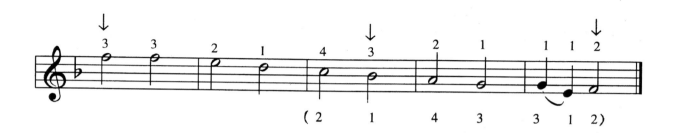

Etude in F Major

Moderato Swoveland

The G Major Scale

The key of G Major has one sharp: F♯.

Two Octave Scale

Three Octave Scale

G Major Arpeggio Three Octaves

Etude in G Major

Moderato   Swoveland

The A Minor Scale
One Octave

The A Melodic Minor key has: Ascending F♯ and G♯

Descending F♮ and G♮.

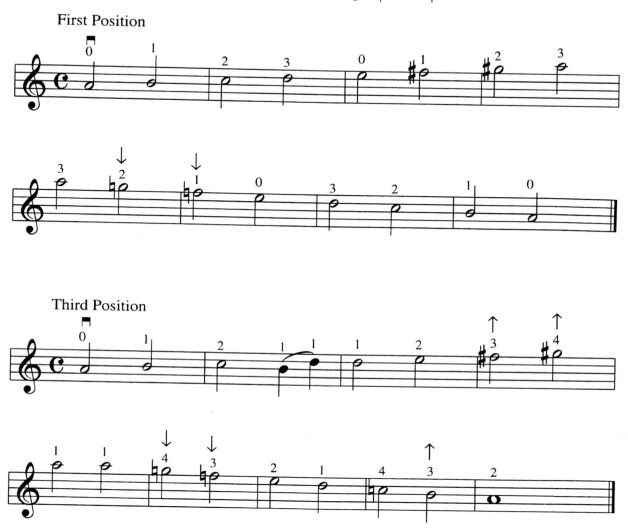

Scale Exercise: Match G with open G.

Etude in A Minor

Moderato   Swoveland

Exercises in A Minor
Preparations for the Vivaldi Concerto

Moderato

Swoveland

Exercise No. 1 In the style of Vivaldi.

Exercise No. 2

Great Music at Your Fingertips